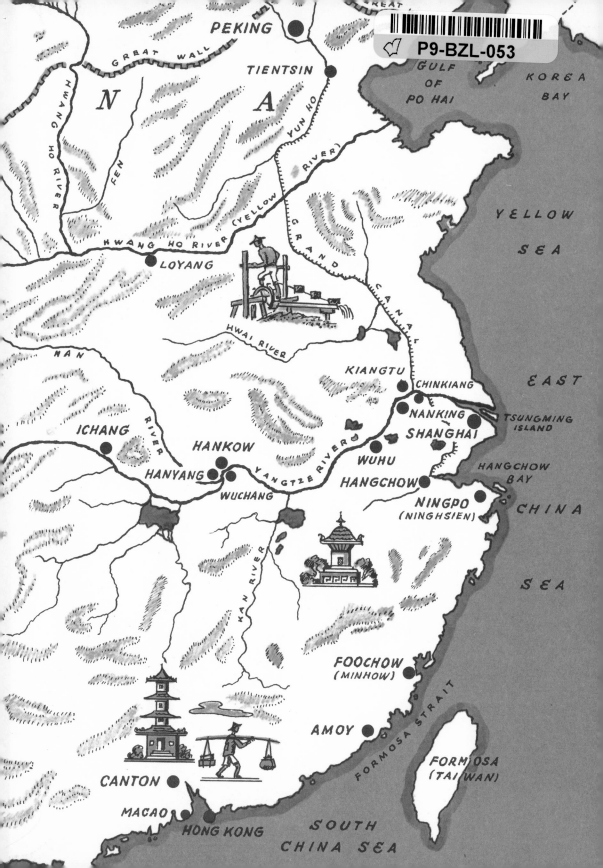

PEKING

GREAT WALL

TIENTSIN

N   A

HWANG HO RIVER

FEN

YUN HO RIVER

GULF OF PO HAI

KOREA BAY

HWANG HO RIVER (YELLOW)

LOYANG

GRAND CANAL

HWAI RIVER

NAN

RIVER

KIANGTU

CHINKIANG

NANKING

SHANGHAI

YELLOW SEA

EAST

TSUNGMING ISLAND

ICHANG

HANKOW

HANYANG

WUCHANG

YANGTZE RIVER

WUHU

HANGCHOW

HANGCHOW BAY

KAN RIVER

NINGPO (NINGHSIEN)

CHINA

SEA

FOOCHOW (MINHOW)

AMOY

FORMOSA STRAIT

CANTON

MACAO

HONG KONG

FORMOSA (TAIWAN)

SOUTH CHINA SEA

THE Yangtze

CHINA'S RIVER HIGHWAY

the

YANGTZE

China's River Highway

by Cornelia Spencer

Illustrations by Kurt Wiese
Maps by Fred Kliem

GARRARD PUBLISHING COMPANY
CHAMPAIGN, ILLINOIS

THIS BOOK WAS EDITED AND DESIGNED
UNDER THE SUPERVISION OF NANCY LARRICK, ED.D.

For reading the manuscript of this book and
checking the accuracy of its content, the author and
editor are grateful to Dr. Tien-yi Li, Professor of
Chinese Literature and Culture, Yale University.

Yangtze River

Contents

Dragon

1. The Dragon King

Sixty years ago in China a drug store was a curious place. All sorts of queer "drugs," seen in no other land, filled the small drawers that lined the walls.

One day a German traveler opened a drawer and found it full of animal teeth.

"What are these for?" he asked in surprise.

"Ah, dragons' bones," the druggist answered. And he went on to explain. Ground to a powder and drunk down with tea, dragons' bones were sure cure for fever, swellings, madness, liver trouble, malaria, and a whole string of other ills.

7

This porcelain dragon is one of nine on a screen at the Winter Palace, Peking, China. The screen is 20 feet high and 100 feet long.

I tell this story of dragons' bones here only to point out that in China a dragon was not thought of as an evil creature. He was no monster from whose claws maidens had to be rescued by shining knights. Dragons were kindly disposed toward man—so kindly that even their bones were a powerful medicine.

Of all the dragon stories told in China, the most famous are about the Dragon King. As a rule, this great dragon was the friend of man. But every once in a while he went on a rampage and tried to swallow the moon. That caused an eclipse. For thousands of years the people of China beat drums and tin pans at such times, or popped firecrackers, to frighten the Dragon King away. They always succeeded.

Some of the stories tell us that the Dragon King liked to curl up in the clouds. At other times it was his custom to sprawl out under a town. But his favorite resting place was near water. He loved to stretch his length beneath a river.

The Chinese people used to hold a yearly

The Dragon King liked to curl up in the clouds.

Dragon Boat Festival. After dark, hundreds of little lanterns were set afloat on the rivers and lakes, and dragon boat races were held.

Now, why should dragons be connected with water? In time of flood, why should the Chinese have thought that the dragons were angry?

I cannot tell you—nobody knows the answer. But one thing is sure. The people of China firmly believed that the Dragon King controlled the waters of their land. It seems an odd notion to us. And yet when you fly over the Yangtze, the idea of a dragon does indeed come to your mind.

9

For the great river, winding through the heart of China, looks very much like a dragon. Its long tail is tangled among the snowy mountains of Tibet. Its hind end is squeezed between cliffs and narrow passes. The monster twists and struggles, making rapids and deep, dangerous whirlpools. Its middle is more relaxed. Lazily it spreads itself between rich green plains. Patchwork farms, emerald hills and tree-shaded villages fringe it now. As the great dragon stretches its chest and shoulders toward the sea, towns big and small lean against its sides. At the coast a vast sky-scraper city rests upon the dragon's brow.

This is Shanghai, the great port of China. Here stands one of the six largest cities on earth. Shanghai is a jeweled crown for the mighty dragon that is the Yangtze.

Shanghai, China's largest city, handles vast amounts of products from local villages.

Street

2. China's Main Street

The Yangtze is not the longest river in the world. That honor belongs to the Nile. Nor is the Yangtze the most powerful. The Amazon is a far mightier river, carrying as it does one-fifth of all the fresh water in the world. But everyone will agree that the Yangtze is the most important. For it affects the lives of more people than any other. In the Yangtze basin live two hundred million human beings, one-tenth of the human race.

Many of these millions do not call the river Yangtze. They call it *Kiang*. That means "The River." Or they say *Ta Kiang*, "Great River." Or

12

Chang Kiang, "Long River." Everybody knows which river they mean because this waterway is China's Main Street. It runs right across the land from west to east, cutting the country in two equal parts. China has few railways and very few flyways. Fleets of heavily loaded trucks do not ply the highways as in our land. So the river is China's highway. Half the goods that travel through the country move along the Yangtze.

But the Yangtze is not only China's Main Street. It is the great agricultural river of China. Look down from your plane and you will see a network of irrigation ditches on either side of the Yangtze. You will see farmers working tread wheels to pump water into the wood-lined ditches. In all the center of the country, Yangtze water reaches out to the crops.

Bales of rice and other products are awaiting shipment down the Yangtze to market.

One big reason why this river is China's Main Street is that many navigable streams and rivers flow into it. These tributaries not only feed water into the main highway. They are streets through which goods can travel to the Yangtze from the provinces and back again. One tributary is the Kan River in Kiangsi Province. Steamships can always go up the Kan for 100 miles. In summer, when the water is high, they can go up 300 miles. As for junks, they can travel some 30,000 miles on the rivers and lakes of the Yangtze system. That is more than the distance around the world.

The Chinese have always been an original people. It is they who invented the compass and gunpowder. They invented printing and engraving. They were the first to manufacture silk and paper and porcelain. So it is not surprising that over the centuries they learned to get the most out of their great river highway.

Shensi and Kansu provinces produce wool, cotton and hides. The Chinese learned to get these things to market in a most unusual way. The goods are made up into bundles around which hides are sewn in a waterproof covering. When the spring floods come, the bundles are dropped into the little streams that lead into the Kialing or the Han River. The bundles float downstream to the collecting centers. There they are fished out and put on board junks to travel the rest of the way to market.

The Chinese have also worked out ways of shipping goods when the water is very low. Some of their junks will float when the water is only two feet deep.

The Chinese make great use of rafts too. Some will float on just one foot of water and yet carry up to 20 tons of goods. Some of the Chinese rafts are immense. They are so big that—until recently—they brought downstream not only goods and families but entire villages. Barbers, tinsmiths and restaurant keepers carried on their trades as the rafts went on their way. At the end of the line, the rafts are broken up for timber. Rafts are an easy way of transporting wood from the forests to treeless plains.

The Yangtze is the great highway of China, but at two seasons of the year the river has very little traffic on it. When the water is at its lowest, traffic almost stops. And when the Yangtze is at fullest flood, traffic almost stops again.

Even in between these times, it is not an easy river to navigate. There are currents, rocks and

A timber raft floating down the Yangtze relies on good luck to avoid collisions. Little steering can be done.

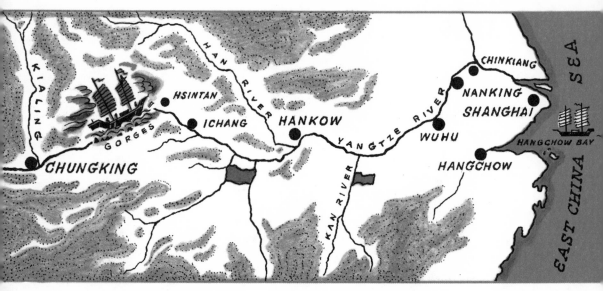

Ichang, 1,000 miles from the East China Sea, marks the beginning of the Yangtze gorges.

gorges. Between Ichang and Chungking the gorges are world-famous not only for their picture-book beauty but also for their wrecks. Probably there is no river journey in the world so dangerous as the 350 miles between Ichang and Chungking. In times past, a good many villages in the gorges lived off these wrecks. The in-habitants didn't fish and didn't farm. They got their living by salvaging goods from boats that were cast on the rocks or broken in the rapids.

18

Some eighty miles up from Ichang stands the town of Hsintan, which means "New Rapids." Many centuries ago a landslide formed new rapids at this point, and they are perhaps the worst ones along the whole upper Yangtze. A hundred years ago the people of Hsintan, which grew up on this spot, were reported to be living largely off the wrecks. The rapids are so bad that the officials closed that part of the river to traffic between November and April. But the people of Hsintan cleared a channel so that boats could pass during this low-water period. However, they cleared it only enough to let *some* of the boats get through. Wrecks occurred very often, and from these the town got most of its living.

It takes very skillful pilots to guide ships through the gorges. There are constant losses. One out of ten ships is badly damaged. One out of twenty is wrecked altogether. But still the ships go on. In spite of everything, the ships go on. They must—there is no other way. The Yangtze is China's Main Street.

Canal

3. A Network of Canals

Coming from the sea, you know the Yangtze is near long before you see it. The color of the water tells you. It is yellow like the Yellow Sea a little farther to the north. The change of color is due to all the yellow mud the river brings down and dumps into the East China Sea.

For this powerful stream is a great carrier of silt. Each day the Yangtze pours, on the average, almost a cubic mile of soil-laden water into the sea. In a single year it leaves 600 million tons of mud and silt on the shore. The river adds and

20

adds to its delta. Every 70 years it builds its delta another mile out into the sea.

The Yangtze has built an island of 275 square miles, too. In the year 620 this island was just a slender sand bar. By 1220 it was an island large enough to have people living on it. Today the sand bar is Tsungming Island, and a million people live there.

Someday this island may become part of the mainland. It won't be the first time such a thing has happened, for the Yangtze has connected islands to the mainland several times before. Places that are now famous hills were once islands in the river's mouth.

The city called Chinkiang, where I was born and lived as a child, was once a seaport on the East China Sea. Today it is 150 miles inland. The river has piled up 150 miles of yellow silt in front of the old seaport.

The great city of Shanghai stands on soft mud flats made by the river. Its skyscrapers are built on piles because ordinary foundations will not hold.

At its mouth the river is so wide that it is hard to see the opposite shore. But the mouth is getting shallower all the time as the river drops more silt. Every twenty years the river bed rises another twelve inches at the mouth. This, of course, increases the danger of flood. The dikes along the lower course of the river have to be built higher and higher to keep the water out of the lowlands.

The delta is a surprising place. Nowhere in the world are so many man-made waterways so close together. The canals connect the natural little waterways and join all the villages with one another and with Shanghai. From Shanghai you

22

The bridges on the delta make pleasing pictures.

can go 100 miles in any direction by water. You can go from village to village, never getting out of your boat, and often this is the only way you *can* go. There are at least half a million miles of man-made waterways in the delta. Nearly all bridges are humpbacked so that ships can pass under them.

Look down from the air and the delta seems like a city map. The canals are the streets. The fields and villages look like city blocks and buildings, so neat and regular do the Chinese farmers keep their boundaries and banks. If there is no wind, you will see men pulling boats to market as

23

they walk along the towpaths beside the canals. Or you will see them rowing slowly and steadily in their narrow boats. On a breezy day, sails will blossom suddenly on the canals.

I have spent weeks on a Chinese houseboat of the Yangtze Valley, sailing along the canals. It is very exciting to have the sail raised. The bamboo yards creak and squeak going up. The boat tips sharply as it adjusts to the new power. It rights itself under the quick hand of the man at the rudder. Then suddenly it is speeding through the narrow channel of yellow water. You feel as if you were racing through a dry countryside on a track of water. And all around you, behind and in front, sometimes on another canal, other sails are rising above fields and villages.

The canals are not only for transport. They also bring water to the rice paddies and the truck farms which are all beautifully kept. North of the Yangtze soybeans and millet are the main crops. South of the Yangtze rice is king.

Land is so precious that everyone wants to get

24

Water buffaloes help in cultivating the rice fields.

just as much out of it as he possibly can. The farmers seem to watch every leaf on every vegetable, and woe to any duck that stretches out its long neck to grab a bite.

The ducks are a real nuisance here. They are raised by the thousand along the river banks. When they are walked to market in noisy flocks, everything has to get out of their way. Their drivers try to control them with long bamboo switches, but they are not always successful. Truck gardeners run out angrily to defend their vegetables when a troop of ducks is passing by.

This is rich land. The Chinese get two and three crops a year out of it. But that is due partly to the climate. There is no frost here for three hundred days of the year. Snow is rare, and if there is any ice at all, it is paper thin and forms only on still water. Rain usually comes in late spring, and that suits the growing of rice exactly. As for drought, irrigation can take care of that. Only floods are feared, and they are a terror indeed. Floods are China's great sorrow.

*The ducks go to
market on foot.*

This fisher-man uses cormorants to catch fish. While fishing, the birds wear metal collars so they can't swallow the fish. They are trained to bring their catch back to the boat.

4. Through Yangtze Gorges

Thousands and thousands of people in the Yangtze Valley spend all their lives on houseboats. Beside Shanghai and other river towns, whole villages of houseboats lie at anchor. They remind you of trailer camps in our own country. The people on them earn a living by carrying cargo up and down the waterways. Or they fish for a living. Fish are plentiful and of many kinds in the Yangtze, its tributaries and the canals. Fishing is a big trade in the valley. It is also fun.

Even if your home is a boat on the river, washday still comes around.

Many a farmer takes time off to fish and get a little variety into his family's diet.

The houseboats with laundry whipping in the wind and children playing on the deck are very picturesque. But the traffic on the great river is

more impressive. Big ocean-going freighters go as far up as Hankow. River steamers can travel a little way beyond Chungking. Smaller craft go farther still. Junks are everywhere, while the little sampans go weaving in and out. And always the great rafts come down.

From all the branches of the Yangtze, vessels are bringing goods. They go to Shanghai, which is a great manufacturing and distributing center. Or to Hankow, the Pittsburgh of China, 640 miles upstream. Or to Nanking, 200 miles from the mouth. (Nanking has several times been the capital of China and is still a very important place.) Or they go to other big towns on the Yangtze. The vessels are loaded with cotton, silk, vegetable oils, tallow, hides and skins, hemp, tea, bristles, wheat, tobacco, eggs. Up the great river and its tributaries go other steamers and junks carrying manufactured goods.

The steamers have an easier time of it. Because they have extra-powered screws, they can get through the gorges without much trouble. The

31

Unloading a steamer
at Nanking

junks have to struggle through. They must be pulled up by hand, past the rapids, past the whirlpools, past the reefs and the rocks.

Let us see how the junks do it. Let us be passengers on a junk carrying goods from Hankow to Chunking, the great commercial city of Szechwan Province, at the other end of the gorges. It will take courage to make this trip. But I promise you it will be rewarding.

Our captain tells us it will be a quick journey. The river conditions are good, he says. And, what is more, he has the best helmsman on the Yangtze. Did you see the way he steered the junk between Hankow and Ichang, where the sand banks lie? He didn't try to fight the river—he coaxed it. He took the junk back and forth across the channel, knowing it would take twice as long if he "bucked" the river. He will carry us through the gorges fast—in 25 days, traveling from dawn to sunset. Of course, at night we'll stop—nothing moves in the gorges at night.

Twenty-five days to go 350 miles doesn't sound

Steamers have an easier time than the junks going through the Yangtze gorges.

fast to us. But the captain laughs when we say
so. This is the best speed any junk can make.
Why, one time when the river was low and the
winds blew the wrong way, it took him 60 days
to go from Ichang to Chungking.

The captain is proud of his ship. He doesn't
care that it is ugly. All he asks is that it bring

him and his 60 tons of goods to Chungking. His junk is made of cypress wood, which doesn't rot easily, and is built after a design hundreds of years old. It is low, with a square nose and a high stern. It is about 100 feet long by 20 feet wide, and to us it seems very crowded.

The skipper has his family with him—this is their home. He is also carrying a crew of about a hundred men. Some seventy or eighty of them are trackers. We shall soon see them doing their work. They are going to tow the junk through the gorges.

We go toward the tiller to take a look at the helmsman. He smiles but never takes his hands from the 14-foot tiller. Is this young silent fellow the person in whom the captain has such confidence? Certainly he is no engineer. He has no instruments that we can see. Not even a compass. No, he is just a river-trained man. He has been up and down the Yangtze so often that he knows every rock and reef in it. He can "read" the water. That is, he can tell from the look of the surface what lies beneath. And this requires great skill, for the water level in the gorges changes all the time. When sudden rains fall upstream, the river can rise 50 feet in a single day. High-water marks of over 200 feet above normal have been recorded.

But now we have entered the gorges, and our eyes leap to the cliffs. Never have we looked at scenery like this. It is terribly exciting. Cliffs thousands of feet high shut in the narrow, wild, rock-strewn river. Our little junk seems tiny against this background of towering cliffs. It is wonderful to think that for nearly a month we shall be seeing cliffs, ever changing and ever the same. They will be of many colors. Some will be purple, some gray, some bright green with trees and scrub. Some will have tiny terraced farms on them—no bit of fertile ground is unused in China. The farms will look like bits of a green jigsaw puzzle.

We have been so struck by the scene that we haven't noticed men scrambling overboard. These

Trackers provide the power to get the junks through the gorges.

are our trackers. We look up on the nearest cliff,
and there they are strung out one behind another.
They are on a narrow track cut high in the face
of the cliff. From the junk the track, or towpath,
looks no wider than a thread.

Each tracker has a short piece of bamboo rope around his almost naked body. The rope is fastened by a slip knot to the towrope. This is made of braided bamboo and is very strong, but it may break. If it does, the tracker must be quick. He must slip the knot to save himself, else he will be dragged down with the rope.

The men are chanting in singsong. This keeps them in step and pulling together. Three gangers, or boss-men, run up and down the track. They do no pulling. Their job is to keep the trackers moving along once they have started. If they stop, the junk may slip into a strong current and drag them all down to their death. The gangers seem to be very intent on their job, but all the time they are listening. They are getting directions from below—when to move, when to stop.

We are amazed at the way they get their instructions. While we were looking at the cliffs and watching the trackers, a drumbeat was sounding in our ears. We didn't pay any attention to it. But now we follow the sound and see that

A thousand miles up the Yangtze, the scenery is breathtaking and a little frightening.

a drummer is squatting at the foot of the mast with a drum between his knees. The tattoo he beats tells the gangers: "All is well. Keep the trackers moving." Should it be necessary to stop, the drummer will suddenly change his rhythm and the gangers will know.

Our eyes follow the 1200-foot towrope that is fastened to the mast. We notice that far behind the trackers, three men are spread out and they are handling the towrope. Their business is to keep it clear of the rocks and boulders on which it is constantly catching. They work fast, for they must get the rope clear before it wears through.

These are brave fellows. They have taken many a fall and have broken bones. But we can see that there is a job that calls for even more courage than theirs. The men standing on the rocks in the middle of the speeding river do the most dangerous work of all. They, too, keep their eyes on the towrope. When it catches on a rock, they swim through the swirling water and throw the rope clear. Many a time as we watch we see them risking their lives. These are brave men indeed.

We can feel the excitement on board as the junk inches its way along. It is trying to round the point of a great reef. The pilot stands on the foredeck. Beside him a dozen or more men are helping to guide the junk. The pilot gives them orders by gesturing with his hand—his voice wouldn't be heard above the noise of the swirl. And all the time his eyes go from the eddies on one side to the rushing water on the other, then out to the reef again.

The men in the middle of the river help to keep the towrope clear of the rocks.

We take a quick look up at the roof of the deckhouse where the captain has been perched all this time watching. We know how we feel ourselves. So we know that though he told us it would be an easy trip, his heart is in his mouth. He meant comparatively easy, of course, for always there are the rocks and the reefs and the current and the rapids and the whirlpools.

Between Ichang and Chungking there are twenty major rapids, no two of them alike. And the rope can break any time.

But the junk is forging ahead. The trackers bend over until their hands touch the ground. They are straining every ounce of their strength to get the junk around that reef. And there! They have done it! Everybody sighs with relief—and then gets ready for the next danger.

"But this is inhuman work! Is it worth it?" we ask ourselves. And then we remember. "This is China's Main Street. The people really have no choice. At least, not yet."

Many changes are taking place in China. The river steamers that once carried the flags of European nations are all Chinese now. In time more steamers will be built. Someday there will be only steamers on the river between Ichang and Chungking. Then men will no longer be called upon to do work which animals would refuse to do. A time will surely come when trackers are not needed any more.

無
訓
練

Untamed

5. Untamed and Untamable

When we have passed the gorges and reached Chungking, we realize why the Chinese government moved there during the Second World War. The enemy might take other cities on the river, but it could never take Chungking. Chungking was too hard to get to.

Here beyond the gorges, in the Red Basin of Szechwan Province, we are in a sort of oasis. This is a natural garden spot of China. Its red soil is very fertile. There is plenty of water because the Min River runs through this good land to join the Yangtze. Two thousand years ago

The Red Basin of Szechwan Province

a famous Chinese engineer, Li Ping by name, set up a network of irrigation ditches along the Min. Those ditches are still being used to water the red farm lands. Surrounded by high mountains, fifty million people live on this fertile red soil.

Chungking is the great city here. Though ordinary ships can go 300 miles beyond, this is the goal of most of the boats that pass through the gorges. They struggle through all the dangers because Chungking is a great gathering place for riches. The riches come from Szechwan Province and from far beyond.

The ships will take back goatskins and buffalo hides and sheep's wool. Many bundles of bristles will go downstream, too, all nicely sorted according to length and tied in neat bundles. The people who buy them will not know that the bristles come from the wildest pigs of the wildest country. Nor will the perfume makers know about the musk they buy. They will have no idea of the far-off border lands from which this almost priceless stuff comes. Most will never have seen a picture of the antelope that carries this reddish-black powder in a tiny pouch.

To get to Chungking we have gone 1,350 miles from the sea. That is not half the length of the river—which is a surprise after all we have seen. But the other half of the Yangtze is something altogether different. Beyond the Red Basin the Yangtze is untamed and untamable. It is just a mad torrent.

Chungking, leading industrial city of southwest China, is surrounded on three sides by rivers.

Chungking stands 850 feet above the sea. We would have to climb another 16,000 feet to reach the source of the Yangtze. But we could never go up the river. It is not possible. No human being has ever gone all the way.

For the Yangtze springs up in the wild, snow-clad Kunlun Mountains, which cross northern Tibet. It is an old, old river, far older than the mountains. Long ago when the Kunlun Range rose and tilted the river up, the Yangtze began filing its way down. It has cut down through mountains three and a half miles high. For hundreds of miles it runs through the deep, gloomy trench it has carved for itself. That trench is more than two and a half miles deep. The river fills the trench from side to side. It is a prisoner between high prison walls. It rages and foams at being restrained.

The river is not very wide in the canyons. In places it is no more than a few dozen yards across. It rushes, rushes along. The current is frightful. When the snows in the mountains are melting, the swollen stream is full of whirlpools. Some are 30 feet wide. No one can go either up or down this terrifying stream, and yet people do cross it. They cross it in Tibetan round-bottomed skin boats. But before they get to the other side, they may be swept a quarter of a mile downstream.

The easiest way to cross is really by the over-head route. At certain points the mountain people have stretched a rope with a trolley that slides

giddily across. Clinging to the trolley they get over. Even animals are tied on and carried across this way. It is all part of the wild, crude life in these deep, beautiful canyons. Here people raise sheep and goats. They hunt. But farming is hard on these steep slopes and in the narrow slits of valleys.

This is what the Yangtze is like all through Tibet. It is savage here, of no use to anyone. It comes roaring and rushing right to the Red Basin of the next province, Szechwan. And then suddenly it quiets down. All at once it becomes a different stream. The current is still strong, but nothing like what it has been. You can hardly believe it is the same river.

Few people have seen these wild upper parts of the Yangtze, and many in the Yangtze Valley have never even heard of them. Indeed, it is hard to believe this part exists. People who travel up and down China's Main Street have to persuade themselves that there is another half, an uncivilized half, to the river. Those who have gone up through the gorges think they have an idea of what that uncivilized half may be like. But they are mistaken. Even the rapids and whirlpools can give no idea of the wildness of the Yangtze in Tibet. It is really beyond imagining.

One way of transporting goods through the mountains is by mule caravan. The mules are muzzled to prevent their stopping to graze.

Door

6. A Closed Door Opens

Rivers are apt to be places where civilization begins. And that is how it was in China. Civilization started on a river—not on the Yangtze but on the Hwang Ho, China's second longest river. It runs far to the north of China's Main Street. Hwang means yellow and gets its name from the silt it carries. Often the Yellow River is called China's Sorrow because it floods about every other year and causes a disaster.

Perhaps civilization began there because of the rich soil along its banks. Soon men had to work together to control the floods. Legend has it that under the direction of King Yu, who was also a great engineer, they cleared the channel of its yellow sand. That stopped the floods for a time. Twenty-five hundred years ago there was plenty of traffic on the Hwang Ho.

Later on, in the 600s, the people got the idea of joining the north and south of their land by a waterway. They dug a canal to connect the Hwang Ho with the Yangtze. Later still they pushed the canal north toward Peking and south to Hangchow. It was a tremendous project. The Grand Canal was dug entirely by hand and was

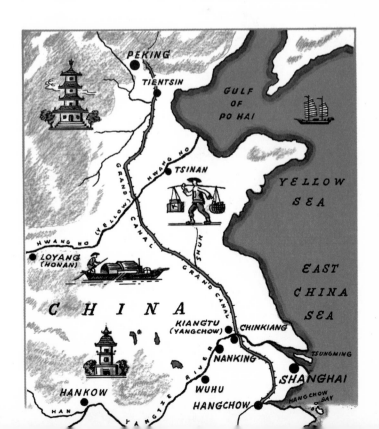

The Grand Canal connects China's two longest rivers—the Hwang Ho and the Yangtze.

1,286 miles long. It was built so well that it is still being used today.

For hundreds of years the Grand Canal was the great north-south highway of China. Goods from far-off places were gathered at either end and taken up or down. Taxes to the emperor went north by the same route, for in those days tribute was paid not in money but in goods and farm products. When taxes were due, barges loaded with rice headed up the Grand Canal to Peking.

This man-made waterway also became the pleasure route of the emperors when they wanted to sail across their broad land. The style they traveled in was fabulous. The three-deck barges were like floating palaces. They sailed from Loyang on the Hwang Ho to Yangchow near the Yangtze, stopping each night at a palace on the shore. For forty days they sailed, and for forty nights they stopped, each night at a palace grander than the last.

The last one, at Yangchow (now Kiangtu),

The Grand Canal, sometimes called "The Transport River," has a total length of over 1,000 miles.

was the most magnificent of all. Here the court amused itself with all sorts of gay doings and lived in the greatest luxury. Yangchow was the city which the Italian traveler Marco Polo governed for the Emperor Kublai Khan.

That was 600 or more years ago. And even

then the Yangtze was China's great highway. Marco Polo was amazed at the traffic on the river. He said there were more boats laden with more precious and costly wares on the Yangtze than sailed on all the rivers of Europe put together. It was his belief that every year as many as 200,000 ships passed up the great river. Some surely carried beautiful silks and porcelains. But much of the cargo was of a practical sort— rice and wheat and soybeans, salt, unrefined sugar and cotton.

There were no steamers then, of course, for it was long before the days of steam. Ocean-going ships, however, slipped in and out of China's

A marble boat which stands near the Summer Palace is typical of the costly imperial palaces along the Grand Canal.

Marco Polo, early explorer, found riches in the East.

harbors. They crossed the neighboring seas to trade with Japan, the Philippines, the Malay Peninsula and Indonesia. They even traded with Ceylon, more than 3,000 miles away.

Europeans knew nothing of all this. They thought China was a savage land. When Marco Polo got back to Italy and told the people about the wonders he had seen, they thought he was making it all up.

Until the 1400's, few white men had touched the shores of China. Daring Portuguese adventurers came then. They were such a rough lot that the

Chinese wouldn't even let them land, but the Portuguese were determined fellows. They kept trying, and after a while they managed to get a toehold near Canton in the south. Their little settlement was called Macao. It was the first Chinese land to be held by a European nation. Soon afterwards, Spanish, Dutch, English and French traders were helping themselves to small places near by. It was the beginning of a long struggle that is only just ending.

By 1784 Americans with their clipper ships had come to China too. They came chiefly to trade for tea, but China's door was also closed to them. They had to stay alongside the Portuguese ships and the British East India Company's ships outside Canton. That was the only city with which China would let them trade.

The foreigners chafed at being kept out of China. Doing business with Canton was all very well, but this was just nibbling at the coast. They wanted to get into the Yangtze Valley. They knew it was a much more important part of China.

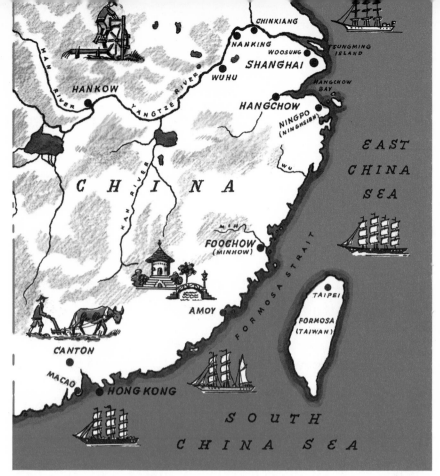

China's seaports tempted the early traders.

That was where most of the people lived. There lay the richest land. There stretched the Yangtze, a watery highway that led straight to the heart of China.

Whenever they could, men of the British East India Company stole north in their ships to look the coast over. On one such trip they spotted an important seaport on a tributary of the Yangtze River right near its mouth. It was Shanghai, the chief marketplace of Eastern Asia. It was guarded, they saw, by a fort at nearby Woosung. If only they could get themselves established at Shanghai! Then the whole interior of the country would be open to them. Shanghai was the key. From there they would trade for all the riches that sailed on the Yangtze.

The British were not the only ones who kept hoping that China would relent. All the foreigners were waiting for China to open her door, but China would not. She would let them trade only with Canton. One reason was that China did not want opium brought into the country. But opium kept coming in.

The Chinese officials grew alarmed. They used every means to stop opium from reaching their people. In 1839 British traders had 20,000 chests of opium on their store-ships off Canton. The Chinese officials wouldn't let them bring the drug ashore.

British ships fire on Chinese junks.

Then the traders tried to smuggle the opium
into the country. The Emperor sent a man named
Lin to Canton to stop the smuggling. Lin obeyed
orders. He had a Boston Tea Party of his own
and began to destroy the opium on British store
ships off Canton.

England had been trying to force China to
open trade with her. Now she declared war when

the opium was seized. A British fleet bombarded Chinese seacoast cities from Canton to Shanghai. From Shanghai the warships sailed up the Yangtze to Nanking, shooting as they went. Then the fleet captured all the junks carrying taxes up the Grand Canal to Peking.

In 1842 the Chinese had to make peace. Britain got $21,000,000 and also took away from China the finest harbor in the Far East: Hong Kong. Also China was forced to open her door, at least part way. From then on, foreigners were allowed to trade not only with Canton but also with Amoy, Foochow, Ningpo and Shanghai. Into these treaty ports opium could be brought freely.

Shanghai

7. Boom in Shanghai

The foreigners had what they wanted now, and they went right to work. Shanghai was the place that interested them most. It was the key to the Yangtze Valley, the door to the greatest riches of China. The foreigners moved in as fast as they could. Shanghai, once a Chinese city for the Chinese people, became something very different.

There was nothing quite like it anywhere else in the world. By far the biggest number of people in Shanghai were still Chinese. They lived behind ancient walls on the fringe of an international city. They had no control over the foreigners.

The foreigners lived in their own International Settlement and French Concession, where they had grants of land for their homes and their businesses. They had their own armed forces to protect them. If a foreigner broke a Chinese law, it didn't matter much. He could not be tried in a Chinese court. The foreigners had their own courts and their own laws. Even if a foreigner made trouble in the native Chinese city, he couldn't be arrested and brought into a Chinese court.

The Chinese people were humbled. No longer were they masters in their own land. In Shanghai it seemed that they lived to serve the Europeans and the Americans. The Emperor was very far away, while the foreigners were very near. The Chinese went about their tasks, always respectful to their foreign masters.

And Shanghai grew and grew. Before the foreigners came, it had been a city of third rank. Twenty years after they moved in, Shanghai was booming. By 1861 half the Chinese goods that

The Bund, part of Shanghai's International Settlement, was one of the city's busiest sections before foreign powers gave up their rights there.

went out into the wide world left by way of Shanghai. It became the first city in China. It grew to be twice the size of its nearest rivals— Peking and Tientsin.

Shanghai became the fifth largest port in the world. It was the gateway through which flowed the tea and silk that came down the tributaries into the Yangtze. And not only that. Shanghai became the center of the north-south trade, of the up-and-down trade of the Chinese coast. And it became a great manufacturing center. The first factory to be built in China was put up in Shanghai. It was a textile mill, the first of many industries to grow up in the city.

Shanghai was a success, which meant that foreign trade in the whole Yangtze Valley was a success. Life was very pleasant and gay indeed for the foreigners. Some lived recklessly in what came to be known as the wickedest city in the world.

But what about the Chinese? Did the big boom which the foreigners started make life better for the Chinese?

For the workers in Shanghai, life was perhaps worse than in any city in the world. There were indeed a few modern factories. But most were built without any thought to the health or safety of the workers. Fires and explosions happened constantly. And each time, many lives were lost because there weren't enough exits or proper stairways. The small shops were the worst. In those that employed just 15 to 100 people, the workers labored under terrible conditions. They were really slaves.

In Shanghai there were no laws that set a limit on how long a person should work or how little he might be paid. Those who worked nine hours a day thought they were lucky, for many people worked twelve. And that was for six or even seven days a week. If a worker didn't produce enough, he was fined. If he was absent because he was sick, he was also fined. His wages were scarcely enough to keep him alive.

Many of the workers were children. And many of them were less than six years old. In some industries where small children worked, special small-sized machinery was built for them.

Most of the children and also many of the young girls in the larger factories didn't come from Shanghai itself. Nor did they get the jobs for themselves. They were brought to the city by contractors who had gone out into the countryside and paid a sum of money to their parents for them. The contractors bought the children's services for three or four years and rented them out to employers.

Some children were apprenticed by their parents to such industries as shipbuilding, woodworking and printing. The food and clothes and shelter these children got were terrible. And the wages they earned were turned over to their parents. That is, if there were any wages, for sometimes the privilege of learning the trade was thought to be pay enough.

A street scene in old Shanghai. Rickshaws, like the one at right, have been outlawed for many years.

The Chinese still carry many loads in the same old way. These steps lead to a ferry across the Yangtze at Hankow.

Factory workers of all ages were very badly off. But the men who pulled the rickshaws were even worse off. They were right down on the bottom.

The rickshaw pullers didn't own the two-wheeled carriages which took the place of taxis in Shanghai. They rented them from contractors. And the contractors rented them from still other contractors. So most of what the pullers earned just passed through their hands—they could keep very little of it. And besides, they had to pay the traffic fines and make good any damage to the rickshaws. Yet the work they did was so hard

67

that their bodies were broken by it while they were still young men in their thirties.

The rickshaw business in Shanghai was what we call a "racket," and the pullers were its victims. The foreigners who carelessly hailed a rickshaw and settled down to enjoy their ride probably had no notion about that. Probably they didn't give a thought to the pullers. How could they? This was Shanghai where the foreigners were the masters. The outsiders had little in common with the barefoot coolies who drew their rickshaws through the streets.

Poppies

8. Poppies Grow in China

And what about opium?

The British had really meant to stop bringing in the drug. Once they were in Shanghai, they planned to exchange British woolen cloth for Chinese silk and tea. But the Chinese couldn't use woolen cloth—the climate of the Yangtze Valley was too warm for wool. So the British went back to the opium trade. It was an easy item to handle and very profitable.

Year by year the opium trade increased. Half the opium that entered the country came through Shanghai, and every foreign steamer took it up

This old engraving, printed in London, shows the British winning a victory in the Opium War.

the river. Opium was unloaded at every river port right up to Chungking. About 70,000 chests of opium were coming in each year. In 1858 a second Opium War broke out. Again China lost. This time she had to open six more "treaty ports" through which opium could be brought in.

"What is the use of importing opium?" the Chinese felt. And they decided to raise their own poppies from which to make their own opium. "If we make our own opium," the government thought, "the people won't buy opium from abroad. Our silver will not go out to foreign countries. Too much is leaving China already."

Whole provinces, or parts of provinces, gave up planting grain and sowed poppy seeds instead. But the government was mistaken. The opium the Chinese made themselves was of poor quality and the foreign opium came in just the same. The only result was that now they had much more than before.

Then in 1906 the Chinese people determined to make a last effort to free themselves of the opium habit.

American traders had brought tons of opium into China. But by this time certain people in the United States were bitterly ashamed of this business. They stood behind China and helped her make an agreement with Britain. Each year for ten years Britain was to bring in ten per cent less Indian opium. And each year for ten years

China was to grow ten per cent less. At the end of that time the battle would be won—no opium would be coming in legally and no poppies would be raised in China. (Smuggling was hard to stop.)

Everything went along fine—almost right to the end. When 1917 came, not a single field of poppies could be found in China. Already the people were getting ready to celebrate their victory. Then just before the ten years were up, the Shanghai Opium Combine found it had 3,000 chests of opium left on its hands. It asked for three months more to sell them. When that was refused, the Combine took things into its own hands. It bribed the Vice-President of the Chinese Republic to buy the 3,000 chests of opium for China.

What a storm broke out then! When the Chinese people learned what had happened, the whole country was in an uproar. In every town mass meetings were held. But the contract to buy the opium had been made; it couldn't be broken. And April 1, 1917, which was to have been the day of celebration throughout the land, became a day of despair. Ten years' work was undone. Though a few months later the 3,000 chests of opium were publicly burned, it was too late. The people had lost hope. They gave up the struggle.

Poppies grew again in China.

The opium poppy shown here is as innocent-looking as the poppies grown in America.

River

9. River Rising!

The Yellow River has always been the sorrow of China. This is not only because it overflows so often. When it floods, the Yellow River has a way of leaving its bed and starting off across the country. Twenty-six times in the memory of man it has gone off and dug a new channel for itself.

The Yangtze is not like this—it doesn't run away. But when it floods, it causes even worse disaster, for China's industry is mainly on the Yangtze.

In summer, when the snows in the Tibetan mountains are melting and the rains are heavy in

74

Workers are filling bamboo "sausages" with stones to strengthen dikes against floods.

the whole basin, the Yangtze generally rises about 50 feet at Hankow. But sometimes it rises much more, and the waters stay high for months. High water on the Yangtze calls for round-the-clock flood-fighting for months.

During this time the summer storms raise great waves. They batter against the dikes, which are already pressed hard by the flood. These waves are very apt to rip holes in the dikes, and the holes must be stopped right away. Otherwise a break-through may take place. Then all the flood fighters on that part of the dike may be swept away.

75

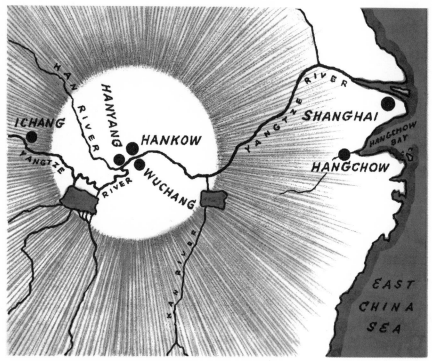

The cities of Hankow, Wuchang, and Hanyang are clustered together at the point where the Han River joins the Yangtze. They are called the Han Cities, or Wuhan.

In 1931 there was a great Yangtze flood. At the place where the Han River joins the Yangtze, the water that summer got up to 92 feet 9 inches. And when it broke through the dike, the disaster was frightful. In this area, which is called Wuhan, there are three industrial cities — Hankow,

Wuchang, and Hanyang. The suffering was beyond the worst nightmare. Help came from many countries. But it was only a drop of what was needed. Sixty million people needed help. During that flood and the hungry winter that followed, millions died.

1931 was an unhappy time for China. The Japanese had seized her northeastern provinces. Worried Chinese government officials didn't do much about helping the flood victims. "Let the International Relief Commission take care of them!" was the attitude.

Some selfish officials were even interested in only one thing: how they could make money out of the disaster. The whole city of Hankow was full of water, yet they were thinking about getting rich. They knew that famine would follow the flood so they bought up grain. They would sell it later at high prices.

When the flood waters broke through the dike at Hankow, those in charge said, "There is still the railroad embankment." But the railway embankment gave way too, and the city was filled with water. Then these men gave orders: "Let the water coming into the city be pumped out within the next three days! And have the dike fixed at once!"

But how was it to be done? Except for a few paddle pumps moved by foot and some odd bits of machine pumps, there was no equipment. One of the chief officials had stolen the taxes that were meant for flood work! He had invested the money in opium and shared the profits with the head of the government.

The officials did not help the flood fighters. Indeed, it might be said that the people rebuilt the dikes in spite of them. It seemed that the officials were saying only, "Nothing can be done! Nothing can be done!"

And so, many of the Chinese drowned. When the waters of that flood went down, 1,000 corpses were collected in three or four days in Wuhan. How many were carried off by the river will never be known.

Hankow residents try to recover their belongings after the Yangtze burst through the dikes.

In Hankow the people living on upper floors could go on living where they were. But the workers in their low cottages became refugees. They were pushed around as if they were enemies —by soldiers at the point of bayonets. Meantime those who had remained in Hankow could scarcely live, for prices of all necessary things had soared.

In the flood of 1931 many starved while a few made fortunes.

*   *   *

In 1949 the Communist Party took over the government and established the People's Republic of China. They had big hopes. One of the first things the Communists planned was a series of projects that would put an end to the floods. Those same projects would make it possible to irrigate new land, which would mean bigger crops. For in China when you irrigate an acre of land, the crop is almost half again as large.

The government was willing to spend a great deal of money on these projects, and the results showed it. Between 1949 and 1952 the people raised nearly 500 miles of dikes along the lower part of the Yellow River. They built over six million small dikes and ditches and built or rebuilt 250 big irrigation projects. They installed seven and a half million water wheels and power pumps. They dug 800,000 wells. Nine million more acres were brought under irrigation.

A carefully tended, irrigated rice field means more food for more people. Weeding, which is what these workers are doing, is done by hand.

By 1955 all the river dikes in the country were in good shape. And meantime some very large projects had been started. One was on the Hwai River, which is about halfway between the Yangtze and the Hwang Ho. The Hwai had a dreadful record of floods. It had overflowed its banks 70 times in 100 years.

In 1950, the Chinese leader, Mao Tse-tung, called on the people to tame the Hwai. Over four and a half million peasants went to work with 40,000 government workers and 16,000 engineers and technicians. They dredged 1,800 miles of the river. They built canals and a movable dam, three reservoirs and fifteen basins to drain off the river water and hold it back. The river Hwai would flood no more. And besides, more land would be irrigated, transportation would be better, and electricity would be produced.

During this time a start was made toward taming the Yangtze too. In the middle Yangtze Valley, a great basin was built into which water could be drawn off from the river. The Tsing Kiang Flood Detention Basin was finished in 1952, and two years later it served the country well. Alone it could not keep the river from overflowing, nor was it expected that it would. But it did its part.

As soon as the water reached 182 feet at Ichang, the 54 great entrance doors of the basin

In day and night shifts, 45,000 Chinese peasants are building a dam. Each one can carry 100 pounds of earth at a time in the baskets connected by bamboo poles.

were opened and water was drawn off and trapped behind them. Engineers held their breath when the first flood crest came. But the Tsing Kiang Dike held. It stood up while five flood crests passed by. In 1931 Wuhan was flooded for four months. In 1954 it wasn't flooded at all. Though in other places the river overflowed, the precious industries of the People's Republic of China were saved.

Flood

10. Flood Fighters Win

The Yangtze in full flood is something so big, so wild, that words cannot describe it. You have to see it to understand its power. In 1954 the Yangtze broke its record—it rose higher than it had ever done before. But this time the government and the people were ready. Over the years the people had learned that floods could be controlled. Now they were organized to fight high water.

The army was sent in to work alongside the people with shovel and spade. Time and again soldiers risked their lives to save people in danger or to prevent their work from being washed away.

The worst disaster area was in the province of Hupeh, and there many people had to be taken out by steamer or boat. Government workers helped them in every way. In one place soldiers held up a tottering bridge with their own bodies while the villagers walked over. Once while people were being moved out, the railway on the south side of the river became flooded. Railway workers labored night and day to raise the railway bed

above the level of the flood so the line could be opened again.

In 1931 everything had been topsy-turvy in Wuhan. Corpses were floating through the streets. But in the flood of 1954 life went on as usual. The stores kept on doing business while prices remained steady. Schools and places of amusement stayed open. Work on the first span of the bridge that would one day cross the Yangtze never stopped. Most important, industry kept going. Factory workers could see the river swirling madly on the other side of the dikes. Yet they kept working all through the flood.

For Wuhan had not waited until things were critical. In early summer when the rains got heavy, reports began to come in of a great rise in the upper part of the river. Behind the three-mile dike of Wuhan were tens of thousands of people. They must be protected as well as the industries of the three Wuhan cities. It could not be enough merely to strengthen the dike.

An army of workers was organized to build a

strong new dike and also an embankment behind the old dike. Thousands of tons of material were brought for this work from three and more miles away.

On July 1, heavy rains were falling and the river was rising fast. Then a break in the dike was reported. A protecting dike had to be built right away, that very night. So the flood workers slogged in the rain. Trucks carrying materials got bogged down as they came near the dike. But inside of two hours strips of sheet metal were laid over the muddy approach. Trucks could come right up to the spot where their earth was needed. The highways were full of trucks rushing up with earth. Boats brought it along the swollen Yangtze and the river Han. Carriers with baskets unloaded the earth at top speed. Earth moved toward the dike all through the night.

Women worked alongside the men. Those who weren't strong enough to carry loads sewed up bags of earth or spread it as it was dumped. Old women who could do nothing else took care of

little children, while the bigger children carried meals to the 200,000 flood fighters. Everyone was doing something to keep the water out. "If necessary, we will move a couple of hills right on to the dike to stand on guard against the waters," the flood fighters said.

And the dikes rose. Once they had seemed not much higher than a man. Now they towered like city walls.

For 100 days the people fought to keep the water out of Wuhan. The railway workers had to raise the railroad bed five times. When a highway was covered by water, army men built a bridge to take its place.

Students worked on the dikes just like anybody else. In their wide straw hats, shorts and sandals, the high school boys looked like ordinary workers. Children made rope for flood work. High school girls washed clothes for the flood fighters. The Honan opera and other troupes came to entertain the workers in their leisure time.

It seemed as if this Yangtze flood was every-

Floods are everybody's business so all must share the work of building protection.

body's business. From every part of the country help came. Trucks, pumps, locomotives, supplies came into Hankow. Then as winter approached the government sent grain and padded clothes.

It seemed like a miracle, but Wuhan was saved.

Down the river, 200 miles from the raging sea that was the river's mouth, Nanking was also fighting to keep the water out. And there, too, the army was in the forefront. Day and night soldiers worked with the flood fighters to hold the river back.

And Nanking, too, stayed dry.

Future

11. Eyes on the Future

After the flood was over and things were normal again, the government took up its master plan for taming the rivers of China. That plan is so daring that it takes one's breath away. Just the plan for the Yellow River is staggering. It is called the Staircase Plan because its chief project is to build 46 dams on the main river. The river levels will form a staircase. But this is only part. In 1957 work began on a dam in the Sanmen gorge. It will back up a great lake and give the country tremendous electrical power.

There are plans for the Yangtze too. On its

tributary, the Han, a great reservoir is being built. It will irrigate nearly two million acres of land and provide much electricity. In the Ichang gorge, east of Chungking, work has started on a dam that will be the largest in the world. It will produce more than twelve times the electric power made by our own Grand Coulee dam.

Today engineers are the heroes in China. The plans they have drawn up are being carried

The first of its kind on the Yangtze, this bridge at Wuhan provides for trains, automobiles, and pedestrians.

out with confidence. The people of China are determined to turn the Hwang Ho from a river of sorrow to a river of joy. They are even more certain that they will tame the Yangtze.

China's Main Street has a great future if plans are carried out. Every year the busy cities on its shores will become more important. More and more tons of manufactured goods will travel up the Yangtze and its tributaries. Surplus grain from Szechwan and other provinces can be shipped to Shanghai for people who live in the coastal cities. And soon there will be vast stores of electric power.

Shanghai, the city where China was once humbled, is no longer a place of shame. Foreigners are masters there no more. At present its face is turned inland. Shanghai looks toward Asia. But someday it will face the other way as well, and then the Yangtze will really come into its own. Then it will be not only China's great inland waterway. It will be a highway that leads China out into the world.

Picture Credits

Photographs, old prints and engravings have been made available for this book through the following sources:

Brown Brothers: Jacket, p. 41, 55, 66

Culver Pictures, Inc.: p. 59, 70

Eastfoto: p. 2, 14, 25, 26, 46, 53, 81, 92

European: p. 30

Ewing Galloway: p. 17, 28, 37, 39, 49, 63

Free Lance Photographers Guild, Inc.: p. 54, 79

Norman Gordon from Black Star: p. 67

Natori from Black Star: p. 33

P.I.P. photos by Der Stern: p. 11, 83, 88

L. Tager from Black Star: p. 6

Wide World: p. 29, 75

Index

Meet the Author

CORNELIA SPENCER, who was born and raised in China, brings to this book a real interest in the Chinese people and a sound background for writing about them. Miss Spencer did her college work in the United States, after which she returned to China and did not leave there to settle in America until 1935. She now lives in Bethesda, Maryland.

Miss Spencer's main interest has been in factual books for young people, although she has also published novels. Many of her books have been about Eastern countries—China, Japan, the Philippine Islands and India. She has written a number of biographies of interesting personalities—the Soong sisters, Prime Minister Nehru, Ambassador Carlos Romulo, former President Harry Truman, and Pearl Buck.

In reply to the question "Why do you write?" Miss Spencer answers "I write when I cannot keep from it—when an idea has taken hold of me." She adds, "Writing is hard work because it is creating. Because it is creating, it is magnificent fun."

C H I

GREAT WALL

HWANG HO RIVER

KUNLUN
MOUNTAINS

HWANG HO RIVER

HWANGHO RIVER

YANGTZE RIVER

KIALING RIVER

T I B E T

YALUNG RIVER

YANGTZE RIVER

MIN RIVER

CHUNKING

MIN RIVER

I N D I A

YALUNG RIVER

YANGTZE RIVER

YALUNG RIVER

B U R M A

V I E T N A M